ESL Lesson Plans

An ESL Teacher's Essential Guide to Lesson Planning, Including Samples and Ideas

by Janie Espinal

Table of Contents

Introduction

Due to globalization, the ability to converse in English has become an incredibly important skill to possess. Business people, students, and the general public alike have become increasingly aware of the advantages provided by English literacy, and are therefore willing to go to great lengths to become proficient in the language.

ESL stands for "English as a Second Language." ESL teachers teach the English language to non-native English speakers all over the world. Thus, English becomes the student's second language. Due to the demand created by folks yearning to be proficient in English, a job market was created for individuals that can teach English to non-native speakers.

While teaching ESL can be challenging, it can also be a very fulfilling experience. This book is designed to help you, the ESL teacher, become better equipped to create enjoyable and effective ESL lessons for your students. Here, you'll learn everything that you need to know to plan great lessons for your classes so that you and your students can make learning English easy, stress-free, and fun.

Chapter 1: Understanding the ESL Students

In the English Academy where I taught for five years, a new batch of Korean, Japanese, or Chinese students arrived every month. A batch could be composed of 80 to 150 students at a time. Most of the students were adults, but some were still in elementary school, middle school, or high school. Their English proficiency would normally range from zero-English to more advanced. Obviously, there should be a system to put students of the same English proficiency together. Here are some tips for any new ESL teacher about getting to know your students' English level. Whether your students belong to the beginner, intermediate, or advanced groups; if you know this information, you can create ESL lesson plans that are suitable for your students' English proficiency.

Step 1: Separate Children and Adult Learners

Normally, children learners are separated from adult learners regardless of their English level. An English Academy must have separate programs for children and adults. Mixing students from different age groups can be complicated and could affect the students' learning. Teaching children English and teaching adults English can be very different, and every ESL teacher will need special training to do both. As a result, there are ESL teachers assigned specifically to children and there are those who specialize in teaching adult learners.

Step 2: Placement Tests

A placement test is specifically created in order to help ESL teachers determine the English proficiency of an ESL student. The test is normally composed of questions that target the four macro skills, namely: Reading, Speaking, Listening, and Writing. Based on the test scores, every new ESL learner can be classified as a Beginner, Intermediate, or Advanced. Without a placement test, it can be difficult to know how much English your new students can speak or understand. This test works very well for schools that have a big number of students.

Step 3: Assigning English Levels

Classifying your students as Beginner, Intermediate, and Advanced is very important. This is the basis for your lesson plans. ESL teachers must always create lessons that are suitable for their students' English proficiency. Otherwise, the students will have a tough time learning and the teacher will have a frustrating time teaching. To create more accuracy in the placement process, the Beginner, Intermediate, and Advanced students can further be subdivided into two levels: low and high. Doing this creates a six-level program for the students to complete.

All ESL students have a study plan period in mind, and whether they have a short-term study plan such as 2-3 months or a long-term study plan such as 4-6 months, they can have levels to advance towards. It is very rare to have new ESL students start in the Advanced levels, but in case this happens and they have a long-term study plan, the ESL teacher can always create special lessons for these more advanced students.

Six Levels Recommended for Long-Term ESL Students

Level 1: Low Beginner
Level 2: High Beginner
Level 3: Low Intermediate
Level 4: High Intermediate
Level 5: Low Advanced
Level 6: High Advanced

Students' levels may or may not be accurate. Remember that these classifications were based on the test scores from the placement test alone. Test scores can be subjective and many new ESL students take the test as soon as they arrive in the English Academy. Most of them are tired, hungry, or too nervous. Therefore, the placement test scores should not be the only basis for determining a student's English proficiency.

Step 4: Teacher's Assessment

Once the students' levels of proficiency have been determined, it becomes easier for any ESL teacher to create lessons and plan his/her classes. But, as mentioned, the placement test should not be the exclusive factor used in determining the students' English proficiency. During their actual classes, ESL teachers can make further assessments of their students English speaking ability, comprehension, listening, reading, and writing. If a teacher sees that a student is in the wrong level, then she can make recommendations for that student to be placed in the right level. More importantly, the teacher can create lessons that will match the student's English proficiency.

Step 5: Creating Lesson Plans for Different Levels

ESL teachers can be assigned to teach one level or multiple levels. It is important for a teacher to create lesson plans that are suitable for every level she teaches. ESL lesson plans should be based on the students' English proficiency. A teacher can't use the same lesson plan that she used for the advanced level again for her beginner students without altering it. Conversely, a lesson for beginners can't be used for the intermediate and the advanced students.

Chapter 2: Creating ESL Lesson Plans

The ESL Lesson plan is much like the regular lesson plan. It has the basic parts such as the Lesson Title, Objective, Warm-Up Activity, Lesson Proper, Assessment, and Application.

Parts of the ESL Lesson Plan

Lesson Title

Having a title for your lesson gives you a general idea of what the lesson is about. An ESL teacher can locate any lesson in her book quickly when these are named properly.

Lesson Objective

ESL teachers need to set an objective for every lesson. A teacher needs to write down one specific goal that she wants to achieve for the class. When setting objectives for your lessons, it is recommended that you follow the SMART guide for creating objectives. The acronym SMART stands for Specific, Measurable,

11

Assignable, Realistic, and Time-Related. Both the teacher and his/her students can benefit from clear lesson objectives.

Target Areas

Most ESL lessons have a specific target areas. Students want to learn about grammar, idioms, and expressions from their teachers. So in your lesson plan, indicate what specific topic in the English language you will be teaching your students. For instance, you can write topics like Phrasal Verbs, The Past Perfect Tense, or Prepositions for your target areas.

Materials

When teaching ESL, teachers need a wide array of teaching and learning materials. These will make learning a new language fun for your students and teaching more effective for you too. Audio, visual, and multi-media can all be very helpful for teachers and students. To promote active listening skills a teacher can use recorders, audio players, and headphones. Pictures, sound clips, and videos are only some of the materials that ESL teachers can use to develop the visual perceptual skills needed for reading. In your lesson plan, you will need to indicate all the materials that you will need for every lesson.

Warm-Up Activity

This is a short activity to introduce the lesson to the students. It also helps to captivate the students' interest for the day's lesson. For the warm-up activity, ESL teachers need to be creative and they should not limit themselves to the classroom. If the lesson is about adjectives, then a good warm-up activity would be to go outside and describe the things they see. However, teachers should be wary of warm-up activities that can be too distracting or too tiring for the students.

Lesson Proper

This is where the ESL teacher introduces new information to her students. She will discuss her main points and allow her students to ask questions in case some points are unclear. If her topic for the day is Linking Verbs, then she will need to give a short lecture on the proper usage of Linking Verbs. She will need to explain the rules to Linking Verb usage so that her students can understand it and be able to use this knowledge to construct grammatically correct sentences. An ESL teacher should always incorporate the students' prior knowledge into her introduction of new knowledge. Start with what your students know and build on it.

Assessment

The assessment part of your lesson occurs when the teacher checks for comprehension. She can either give quizzes or an activity to confirm whether the students already understood the lesson or will need more explanation and exercises. The assessment should be short and basic using a maximum of ten questions. This assessment provides feedback which you will need when planning a follow up lesson.

Application

In this part, ESL students are provided opportunities to use the new information that they have learned. For example, the teacher can prepare an activity where the students get to practice using Linking Verbs in their conversations. The activities for this part in the lesson should also clearly show the students the usefulness of what they've learned in class. Students must be allowed to use this time to gain confidence in their ability to apply the knowledge gained during the lesson.

Chapter 3: ESL Lesson Plans for Beginners

Many students who belong in the Beginner Level have very low English proficiency. Most will not be able to speak or understand any English so it can be a nerve-wracking experience for any student to go to his first one-on-one class. New ESL teachers can also find this very frustrating. In group classes, beginner students will often speak to each other in their own languages. In this case, the ESL teacher should encourage the students to make an effort to use English words for what they need to say. Beginner students are usually allowed to use a dictionary, unlike intermediate and advanced students who are strictly prohibited to use it.

When creating lesson plans for the Beginner Level, ESL teachers need to remember that most students will not understand what she will be saying most of the time. Therefore, it is best to use the most basic vocabulary, simple sentences, and speak slowly and clearly.

Sample Lesson Plan 1 for Beginners — Individual Class

LESSON TITLE:	TODAY I...
LESSON OBJECTIVE:	After this class, the student will successfully be able to form grammatically correct sentences using the SV and SVO sentence patterns.
TARGET AREAS:	Subject-Verb (SV) / Subject-Verb-Object (SVO)
MATERIALS:	Visual Scaffolding: • Photos of friends

TODAY I...

ACTIVITIES & PROCEDURES:

WARM-UP ACTIVITY:

Ask the student to describe their morning. You should encourage the student to talk about the activities they do before coming to class. In this activity, teachers should encourage their students to practice speaking in English.

Write down the sentences made by the student for use later. For instance, when the beginner student is asked about their first day in the language school, they may say sentences like:

> "I eating breakfast." — I eat breakfast.
> "I sleeping."— I sleep.
> "She coffee drink."— She drinks coffee.

LESSON PROPER:

The Subject-Verb (SV) and Subject-Verb-Object (SVO) Sentence Patterns

The sentences that were written from the student's recount will be used in this part of the lesson. You should show these sentences to the student and teach them the correct form. In this part of the lesson, introduce the SV and the SVO basic sentence patterns. Explain that there are other sentence patterns that the student should learn about, but for today, they will tackle these two patterns.

Subject-Verb Pattern

A sentence can be composed of a subject and a verb only. Putting these two words together can create a full sentence and can give complete meaning. The subject can be a noun or a pronoun. The verb can be an action verb or a state verb.

Examples:

I eat.
He sleeps.
Sheila smiles.
This stinks.
It hurts.

Subject-Verb-Object Pattern

The SVO sentence is the composed of a subject, verb, and object. It's a very simple sentence pattern that most beginner students prefer to use. The subject is a noun or a pronoun, the verb is an active verb and the object is always a noun.

Examples:

I eat breakfast.
Tom drinks coffee.
Sally calls Joe.
He brings snacks.
I like bagels.

ASSESSMENT:

Part 1: Fill in the grid with a Subject, Verb, and Object to form the SV and the SVO Pattern. Write 5 sentences for each pattern.

SUBJECT	VERB
1.	
2.	
3.	
4.	
5.	

SUBJECT	VERB	OBJECT
1.		
2.		
3.		
4.		
5.		

APPLICATION:

For this part, ask the student to create a short introduction of themselves. Explain that now that the student is in a foreign country, they may have the opportunity to introduce themselves to a lot of new people. Of course, they will need to do this in English. It will be very useful to know what to say on these occasions.

Allow the student to create sentences and, then, to identify the SV and the SVO sentence patterns in their introduction.

For example:

Hi. My name is Jim. I'm from Japan. I sing. I love music. I like dancing. Nice to meet you!

Ask the student to practice saying his introduction and to introduce himself to another student after the class.

—End of Lesson—

Many new ESL teachers undergo training on how to teach students from different levels. It can be particularly challenging for new ESL teachers to teach in the Beginner Level. The Beginner Level is probably the most difficult level to handle for ESL teachers. The students have low English proficiency and miscommunication between teacher and student is very common. Many students become disheartened at their slow progress, so in addition to teaching English, ESL teachers need to keep their students interested and motivated. Needless to say, ESL teachers assigned to the beginner level must have a great deal of patience and dedication to help their students. When creating lesson plans for Beginner students, a teacher should always use simple vocabulary words and provide clear instructions for activities.

Sample Lesson Plan 2 for Beginners — Small Group Class

LESSON TITLE:	**AROUND THE WORLD**
LESSON OBJECTIVE:	After this class, students will be able to name 15 of the world's major countries and nationalities in English, and use correct forms of the verb *"be"* in the simple present tense.
TARGET AREAS:	Use of *"be"* + *"from"* in the simple present tense, with all subject pronouns in the affirmative, negative, and interrogative forms.
MATERIALS:	Visual Scaffolding: • A world map • Photos of people of the following nationalities in traditional or stereotypical clothes: *Australia, Brazil, Canada, China, France, Germany,*

	Italy, Japan, Poland, Russia, South Africa, Spain, Sweden, the U.K., the U.S.

AROUND THE WORLD

ACTIVITIES & PROCEDURES:

WARM-UP ACTIVITY:

Point to different countries on the map and help the students label and pronounce them correctly.

Australia	**Germany**	**South Africa**
Brazil	**Italy**	**Spain**
Canada	**Japan**	**Sweden**
China	**Poland**	**the U.K.**
France	**Russia**	**the U.S.**

LESSON PROPER:

PART 1: Countries and Nationalities

Show the students photos of people from different countries to help them learn and memorize the various nationalities. Note that most nationalities end with "-*an*", "-*ish*", or "-*ese*".

Now fill in the following chart together while you go through the photos a second time.

Country	Nationality	Country	Nationality
Australia	Australian	Poland	Polish
Brazil	Brazilian	Russia	Russian
Canada	Canadian	South Africa	South
China	Chinese	Spain	African
France	French	Sweden	Spanish
Germany	German	the U.K.	Swedish
Italy	Italian	the U.S.	British
Japan	Japanese		American

PART 2: Pronouns *I, you, we, they* + *"be"*...

Ask the students to read the following example sentences aloud, first the full form and then the shortened form. Remember to correct their pronunciation.

+	I **am** from Sweden. You **are** from the U.K. We **are** from Russia. They **are** from China.	**I'm** from Sweden. **You're** from the U.K. **We're** from Russia. **They're** from China.
−	I **am** **not** from France. You **are** **not** from Japan. We **are not** from the U.S. They **are** **not** from Canada.	**I'm** **not** from France. You **aren't** from Japan. We **aren't** from the U.S. They **aren't** from Canada.
?	**Are** **you** from Germany? **Are** **they** from Spain? **Are** **you** **not** from Brazil? **Are** **they** **not** from South Africa?	**Are** **you** from Germany? **Are** **they** from Spain? **Aren't** **you** from Brazil? **Aren't** **they** from South Africa?

ASSESSMENT:

Let the students first work through the following exercises alone or with a partner. Then go through them together as a group.

A. + Affirmative

Explain to the students that we often shorten *"I am"* to *"I'm"*, *"you are"* to *"you're"*, *"we are"* to *"we're"*, and *"they are"* to *"they're"* in English.

Exercise: *Fill in the missing word in the conversation.*

1. I___ from France.
2. Oh right, you___ French! This is my wife. We___ from Russia.
3. Really? You___ Russian. What about those people over there?
4. I'm not sure. I think they___ from Australia.

B. – Negative

Explain to the students that we often shorten *"I am not"* to *"I'm not"*, *"you are not"* to *"you aren't"*, *"we are not"* to *"we aren't"*, and *"they are not"* to *"they aren't"* in English.

Exercise: Fill in the missing word(s) in the conversation in their negative form.

1. I___ ___ from Germany.
2. Oh right, you ___ German. My wife and I ___ from Germany either.
3. What about them? They ___ from Canada, are they?
4. No, they ___ Canadian, I think they___ French.

C. ? Interrogative

Exercise: Fill in the missing word(s) in the conversation.

1. ___ you from South Africa?
2. No I___ ___ from South Africa, I'm from France.
3. What about your wife and her friend? ___ they from Australia?

31

4. No, we ___ from Australia, we're all from the U.K.

PART 3: Pronouns _He, she, it_ + "_be_"...

Ask the students to read the following sentences aloud while you help them with their pronunciation.

+	He **is** from Japan. She **is** from the U.K. This toy **is** from China.	He**'s** from Japan. She**'s** from the U.K. This toy**'s** from China.
−	He **is not** from Italy. She **is not** from Poland. It **is not** from Australia.	He **isn't** from Italy. She **isn't** from Poland. It **isn't** from Australia.
?	**Is he** from France? **Is she not** from Germany? **Is it not** from the United States?	**Is he** from France? **Isn't** she from Germany? **Isn't** it from the United States?

32

ASSESSMENT:

Let the students work through the following exercises alone or with a partner. Then go through them together as a group.

A. + Affirmative

Explain to the students that in the affirmative form, we often shorten *"he is"* to *"he's"*, *"she is"* to *"she's"* and *"it is"* to *"it's"* in English, as shown in the grammar box.

Fill in the missing word in the conversation.

1. Where___ he from?
2. He___ from Spain.
3. Really? He___ not from the United States.
4. No, but his wife___ American.

B. – Negative

Explain to the students that in the negative form, we often shorten *"he is not"* to *"he isn't"*, *"she is not"* to *"she isn't"* and *"it is not"* to *"it isn't"* in English, as shown in the grammar box.

Fill in the missing word in the conversation. Use the negative form.

1. Where's she from? South Africa?
2. She ___ from South Africa, I think she's from Australia.
3. No, she ___ from Australia. He ___ from Australia either.
4. Right, their home country ___ South Africa or Australia.

C. ? Interrogative

Explain to the students that in the interrogative form, we usually shorten "*is he not*" to "*isn't he*", "*is she not*" to "*isn't she*" and "*is it not*" to "*isn't it*" in English, as shown in the grammar box.

Fill in the missing word in the conversation.

1. I like that radio. Where___ it from?
2. I think it___ from Japan.
3. ___ it from China? It says "Made in China" on the side.
4. You___ right. It ___ from Japan, ___ from China.

34

APPLICATION:

Working with a partner, ask the students to read the following paragraph aloud. They should substitute the underlined words to describe themselves, a friend, the teacher, and then their partner.

- My name is <u>Peter</u>. I'm not from <u>France</u>, I'm from <u>Poland</u>. My friend <u>David</u> is from Australia. The teacher's name is <u>Paul</u>. He's from <u>Sweden</u>. This is <u>Mary</u>. She isn't from <u>Russia</u>, she's from <u>the U.S.</u>

—End of Lesson—

Sample Lesson Plan 3 for Beginners — Small Group Class

LESSON TITLE:	**FOOD AND DRINK**
LESSON OBJECTIVE:	After this class, the students will be able to name 15 basic foods, use *"there is"* and *"there are"* constructions, and understand countable and uncountable nouns.
TARGET AREAS:	Countable and uncountable nouns, *there is, there are*
MATERIALS:	<u>Visual Scaffolding:</u> • Photos of foods: *a banana, a bunch of grapes, an apple, an orange, a glass of orange juice, a bottle of water, a bowl of fruit, several tomatoes, a roast chicken, several eggs, a bowl of salad, a loaf of bread, a sandwich, a box of cookies, olive oil*

	• Optional photos (nouns): *the Eiffel Tower, a wedding, a spoon, a cat...*

FOOD AND DRINK

ACTIVITIES & PROCEDURES:

WARM-UP ACTIVITY:

Work through the following list of words and help the student improve their pronunciation.

banana	water	salad
grapes	fruit	bread
apple	tomato	sandwich
orange	chicken	cookie
orange juice	egg	olive oil

Now show them alongside various photos and see if the student can match the word to the photo.

LESSON PROPER:

PART 1: What is a noun?

A noun names something. Show the students various photos to demonstrate this concept.

- a person or animal
  e.g. a cat
- a place
  e.g. the Eiffel Tower
- an object
  e.g. a spoon
- an idea
  e.g. two people getting married

Ask the students to choose whether the photo shows a person or animal, a place, an object or an idea.

PART 2: Countable and Uncountable Nouns

Show each of the food photos again. Check whether the students can remember and pronounce the words correctly.

Now ask them to try and identify whether the item is a countable or uncountable noun and write it in the correct box. You can either do this together as a group or allow them to work in pairs first.

Things you can count (countable nouns)	Things you can't count (uncountable nouns)
banana(s)	orange juice
grape(s)	water
apple(s)	fruit
orange(s)	bread
sandwich(es)	salad
cookie(s)	bread
egg(s)	fruit
tomato(es)	olive oil
chicken(s)	grapes

Make sure you teach pronunciation of both singular and plural forms of the countable nouns.

PART 3: "*There is*", "*there are*", and "*some*"

Introduce the students to the concept of "*there is*" for singular countable nouns, "*there are*" for plural countable nouns, and "*there is some*" for uncountable nouns.

* Note that you cannot start a sentence with the word "*have*", as in "*Have two apples*", which is the way many languages express "*there is/are*".

Countable (1)	There is an orange.
Countable (2 or more)	There are two oranges.
Uncountable	There is some orange juice.

Explain to the student that we often shorten "*there is*" to "*there's*" in English.

ASSESSMENT:

Ask the students to sort each of the foods in our list into the correct box and then read the full sentence aloud.

There's one...	There are two...	There's some...
banana(s)	banana(s)	orange juice
grape(s)	grape(s)	water
apple(s)	apple(s)	fruit
orange(s)	orange(s)	bread
sandwich(es)	sandwich(es)	salad
cookie(s)	cookie(s)	bread
egg(s)	egg(s)	fruit
tomato(es)	tomato(es)	olive oil
chicken(s)	chicken(s)	grapes

APPLICATION:

Shopping List Memory Game

Move around the class one at a time asking each student to add an item to the group shopping list, e.g. *"I need to buy: some orange juice, two sandwiches, four eggs, one chicken, some grapes..."* The student must list all of the previous items added to the list. If the student can't remember all of the previous items in order, the list begin

—End of Lesson—

Sample Lesson Plan 4 for Beginners — Individual Class

LESSON TITLE:	**MY FAMILY AND I**
LESSON OBJECTIVE:	After this class, the students will be able to name members of their family and use the present simple tense in its affirmative and negative forms.
TARGET AREAS:	Present Simple Tense
MATERIALS:	Visual Scaffolding: • Photos of family members: *man, woman, boy, girl, old man, old woman* • Photos used for demonstrating verbs: *a person walking (go), a person holding something (have), a person standing in front of a house (live), a person studying (study), a person working (work)*

MY FAMILY AND I

ACTIVITIES & PROCEDURES:

WARM-UP ACTIVITY:

Show the student a series of photos of different family members while introducing the following vocabulary:

boy, girl, man, woman, old man, old woman

Ask the student to repeat each word until they can name all of the people in the photos.

LESSON PROPER:

PART 1: Family Members

Now show two or more photos alongside one another and help the student identify the familial relationship, e.g. father and daughter, brother and sister, grandmother and grandson, husband and wife, etc.

brother, sister, mother, father, son, daughter, parents, children, husband, wife, grandmother, grandfather, grandparents, grandson, granddaughter, grandchildren

PART 2: Simple Present Tense

Introduce the present simple tense for the verb *"be"* with subject pronouns.

I am
we are
you are
he /she / it is
they are

ASSESSMENT

Help the student select the correct form for each of the following sentences.

Exercise: Fill in the missing form of the verb "**be**" in the sentence.

1. Mary __ Peter's mother.
2. Peter and Sara __ Mary's children.
3. I __ Sara's grandmother.
4. David and Mary __ Peter's parents.
5. We are __ David's children.
6. They __ Peter and Sara's grandparents.
7. You __ David's son.
8. Richard __ Sara's grandfather.
9. Jane __ Richard's wife.
10. Sara and Peter __ Richard and Jane's grandchildren.

SPEAKING ACTIVITY

Ask the student to read the following sentences and fill in the blanks with a word of their choice.

- My brother's name is __. He's __ years old.
- My sister's name is __. She's __ years old.
- I'm an only child.
- My mother's name is __.
- My father's name is __.

46

PART 3: Simple Present Tense Verbs – *go, have, live, study, work*

Use the photos as well as your own physical movements to introduce the following verbs:

go, have, live, study, work

+ Affirmative

Ask the student to read the following examples out loud. Remember to help them with their pronunciation.

I, you, we, they...

- I **go** to Queen Mary University.
- I **have** three sisters.
- You **live** in London.
- We **study** medicine.
- They **work** in a hospital.

He, she, it...

- He **goes** to the bank.
- She **has** four brothers.
- He **lives** in Paris.
- She **studies** English.
- He **works** in a school.

Now see if the student can create his/her own sentences using the same format.

Using the same verbs, help the student form sentences in the negative and affirmative forms, first using the pronouns *I, you, we, they*, then using *he, she, it*.

APPLICATION:

The student should now be able to introduce him/herself using the present simple tense and the five new verbs.

Example:

My name is Peter. I am 14 years old. I have two brothers. They are 18 and 22 years old. I live in Paris. I study at Sacred Heart High School. I don't work at the moment.

Ask the student to describe someone they know using the five verbs, as in the following example.

Example:

My brother's name **is** Richard. He's 27 years old. He **has** one daughter. He **lives** in New York. He doesn't **study**. He **works** in a bank.

—End of Lesson—

Chapter 4: Plans for Intermediate Learners

The Intermediate Level is a bit easier to teach than the Beginner Level. The students can understand common English words and phrases and they can actually hold simple conversations with their teachers. They are also able to express themselves coherently without the need to use a dictionary. Nevertheless, the comprehension level of most students in this level is not high, so teachers will still constantly need to explain a lot of things such as idioms, expressions, jokes, etc. All the same, it's more enjoyable to teach Intermediate learners than Beginner students.

In Chapter 3, I provided an example of a formal lesson plan for the Beginner Level. In this chapter, I will show you that there are a variety of ways to teach ESL. Of course, you still need to have a lesson title, a SMART objective, and even a target area, if you like. You can indicate these in your lesson plan. But just to give you an idea how ESL classes can be made so much more fun yet still effective, here is a sample lesson plan for students in the Intermediate Level.

Sample Lesson Plan for Intermediate Students — Individual Classes — Speaking Class

LESSON TITLE:	GIVING ADVICE
LESSON OBJECTIVE:	After this class, the students will be able to correctly use the most common expressions required for giving advice.
TARGET AREAS:	Common Expressions for Giving Advice
MATERIALS:	"Dear Abby" problem situations written on individual cards

GIVING ADVICE

ACTIVITIES & PROCEDURES:

WARM-UP ACTIVITY:

The teacher asks her student if he is familiar with the "Dear Abby" advice column. If so, the teacher initiates a conversation about the people that write Abby and their typical problems.

In case, the student isn't familiar with the popular advice column, the teacher should ask the student if, in his country, there are TV shows, radio programs, or newspaper columns that give advice to its viewers, listeners, and readers. The teacher encourages the student talk for some time about how he thinks advice programs work. This will help the student practice speaking in English. A brief relevant video clip could also be useful.

SPEAKING ACTIVITY:

1. Before the class, the teacher would have prepared problem situations which were written on individual cards. The teacher can

use actual "Dear Abby" problems or she can create problem situations that the student can better relate to.

2. The student will pick one card at a time, read it aloud, and provide advice for the problem. Basically, the student will be Abby, the advice giver. The teacher makes sure that the student understood the problem correctly before he can offer his advice.

3. The teacher will ask various questions to make sure that the student stays engaged in the topics.

4. After the student has provided advice for two problems, the teacher introduces these common expressions and encourages the student to try and use these when he offers his advice.

<u>Common Expressions Used for Giving Advice:</u>

You must...
You'd better...
Why don't you...?
Why not...?
How about...?
You don't have to...
You've got to...
You ought to...
How about...instead of...?
You could...instead of...

5.   Ask the student to offer advice for the rest of the problems.

6.   The teacher corrects any grammar mistakes that the student makes during their discussion.

—End of Lesson—

A lot of students in the Intermediate Level prefer to have Speaking Classes with their individual teachers. Most of the students in this level just want to have more opportunities to practice speaking in English. ESL teachers need to prepare lesson plans for speaking classes and although a target language is not necessary in this type of class; the lesson should always have a clear objective.

Fortunately, the topics for speaking classes are unlimited and a teacher can pick something from the news or even from the student's interests. Many times, the student will suggest a topic that he wants to talk about and the teacher can create a lesson plan around that.

During speaking classes, the ESL student will make a lot of grammar mistakes. ESL teachers should always check the student's sentences. Teachers can correct mistakes verbally or jot down any corrections for the student to see. Teachers need to ask the student whether he/she prefers to be corrected during the conversations or after the discussion.

Sample Lesson Plan for Intermediate Students — Group Speaking Class

LESSON TITLE:	**SIGHTSEEING**
LESSON OBJECTIVE:	After this class, students will be able to name several important landmarks, and recognize the difference between active and passive adjectives.
TARGET AREAS:	Adjectives, active and passive adjectives ending in *–ing* and *–ed*.
MATERIALS:	Visual Scaffolding: • Photos of famous landmarks: *the Eiffel Tower, the Louvre, London Bridge, Big Ben, the Statue of Liberty, the Great Wall of China, the Golden Gate Bridge, the Pyramids of Giza, the Sydney Opera House*

SIGHTSEEING

ACTIVITIES & PROCEDURES:

WARM-UP ACTIVITY:

Show the students the photos of famous landmarks. First, see if they can name the country (and city) that hosts each landmark.

the Eiffel Tower
Paris, France
the Louvre
Paris, France
London Bridge
London, U.K.
Big Ben
London, U.K.
the Statue of Liberty
New York, U.S.A.
the Great Wall of China
Huairou, China
the Golden Gate Bridge
San Francisco, U.S.A.
the Pyramids of Giza
Al Haram, Egypt
the Sydney Opera House
Sydney, Australia

Now go through the landmarks a second time and see how many they can name. Make sure they can pronounce each one correctly.

Continue through the photos until the students can label all of them without prompting. You can also ask students to see how many other famous landmarks they can come up with.

LESSON PROPER:

PART 1: Speaking Practice

Working with a partner, ask students to prepare answers to the following questions.

1. Which city would you most like to visit and why?
2. What kind of things would you do during the day?
3. What would you do in the evening?
4. What kind of accommodation would you prefer and why?
5. Where did you last go on vacation? What do you remember most?

Ask students to read through the following list of adjectives. Help them with their pronunciation.

beautiful	spectacular
famous	huge
thrilling	dazzling
exciting	popular

See how many more adjectives the students can think of to describe famous landmarks. Write them on the board.

Ask students to complete the following exercise with a partner. Make sure they use the new list of adjectives to help them.

- *Choose a world-famous landmark. Discuss with your partner why this particular landmark is so popular.*

PART 2: Active and Passive Adjectives

Explain to the students that certain adjectives have two forms. One with an *–ing* ending and one with an *–ed* ending.

Adjectives ending in –*ing* have an active meaning, for example, "*an exciting town*" interests someone, such as the speaker.

Adjectives ending in –*ed* have a passive meaning, for example, "*She is excited about her vacation*" describes how the vacation makes her feel.

ASSESSMENT

Ask the students to complete the following table in pairs, or you can work through it together as a class.

VERB	ACTIVE ADJECTIVE	PASSIVE ADJECTIVE
to excite to frighten to interest to surprise to fascinate to amaze to thrill to bore to astonish to terrify to shock	surprising	bored shocked

Now, working in pairs, create sentences using both active and passive forms of the adjective.

APPLICATION

Ask the students to tell their partner and then the group about a city they have visited or lived in. Encourage them to use adjectives from the new list. They can use the following sentences to guide them.

- I think _ is a very *interesting* city, because…
- It's *amazing* that _ does/doesn't have…
- It's *surprising* that _ is…
- People who visit _ are often *shocked* when they see…

—End of Lesson—

Sample Lesson Plan for Intermediate Students — Individual Writing Class

LESSON TITLE:	TELLING A STORY
LESSON OBJECTIVE:	After this class, the student will understand the difference between the past simple and past continuous tenses and when to use them.
TARGET AREAS:	Past simple and past continuous tense
MATERIALS:	• Written exercises below • Past tense timeline infographic

TELLING A STORY

ACTIVITIES & PROCEDURES:

WARM-UP ACTIVITY:

Ask the student to try and describe what they did yesterday using the past simple tense.

For example, *"Yesterday, I got up at 7am, then I had breakfast. Then I went to class at 9am and studied English for two hours."*

LESSON PROPER:

PART 1: Review the Past Simple

Ask the student to write the following verbs in their past simple form. Help them to identify which verbs are regular and which are irregular.

Yesterday I __ (**wake up**) at 6am. I __ (**brush**) my teeth, then __ (**take**) a shower and __ (**get dressed**). After that I quickly __ (**make**) breakfast while I __

64

(**watch**) the news on TV. I __ (**have**) bacon, sausages and fried eggs. At 7:30am, I __ (**drive**) to work. I __ (**work**) on a project until 10:30am then __ (**go**) to a staff meeting at 11am. I __ (**talk**) for a while with my boss and co-workers and then __ (**decide**) to have lunch at a nearby Japanese restaurant. I __ (**order**) the sushi and a cold noodle dish. At 1:30pm, I __ (**continue**) working on my project until 4:45pm when I finally __ (**leave**) the office. I __ (**spend**) a few hours eating and drinking with my co-workers at a nearby hotel restaurant. We __ (**chat**) for a while about the project and our client. Then I __ (**head**) back home to get some much needed rest.

PART 2: Introduce the Past Continuous

The past continuous is formed using the verb *be* in the simple past with the verb +*ing*. For example:

> I **was** eat**ing**
> You **were** talk**ing**
> He **was** work**ing**
> We **were** listen**ing**
> She **was** read**ing**
> They **were** sing**ing**

The past continuous is used to describe actions or events in the past, which began in the past and are <u>still happening at the time of speaking</u>. In other words, they express an incomplete action in the past.

For example: **I was eating** a sandwich <u>when</u> my wife called me.

PART 3: Use the Past Simple and Past Continuous Together

Demonstrate the difference between the two tenses using the timeline infographic.

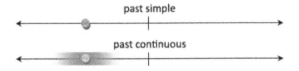

Examples:

- I **was reading** a book when my daughter **arrived**.
- He **was driving** to Chicago when the car **broke down**.

- She **was eating** lunch when her mother **called**.
- We **were walking** to the store when it **started** to rain.
- They **were watching** a movie when the TV **exploded**.

ASSESSMENT

Ask the student to complete the following sentences using the past continuous tense.

I __ (**watch**) the football at a bar when my wife called me.

They __ (**play**) cards when I arrived at the bar.

She __ (**study**) French when I went into her room.

I __ (**eat**) lunch when I heard about the accident.

We __ (**drive**) to my parents house when my father texted me.

APPLICATION

Ask the student to write down a description of his/her day yesterday using both the present simple and present continuous tenses.

They can use the exercise in PART 1 as a guide, but they will need to add additional sentences using the present continuous.

Example:

> I **woke up** at 6am and then **went** to the bathroom to brush my teeth. I **was** in the middle of **taking** a shower when my daughter **shouted** at me to hurry up. As I **was making** my breakfast the toaster **exploded**...

—End of Lesson—

Chapter 5: ESL Lessons for Advanced Learners

Students who have lived in England, Canada, Australia, or in the U.S. for some time may possess advanced English skills. Their grammatical errors are minor and their vocabulary is also advanced. Many of the students in the Advanced Level will still struggle with comprehension so the teacher should always be ready to check any errors. Students in the advanced level are also able to talk faster and can emulate the American or the British accent. Teachers assigned to the advanced level usually teach TOEIC, TOEFL, Business English, or anything that the student requests.

Lesson Plan Ideas for Advanced Learners— Individual Classes

Speaking Class

For speaking classes in the advanced level, ESL teachers can use almost any topic for their lessons without worrying too much that the student might not understand it. Of course, not all students have the same English skills so teachers should always assess every student's English proficiency when creating lesson plans for their classes. Students in the advanced level often prefer to have speaking classes because they are able to practice speaking in English. Discussion and debate are some of the activities that students in the advanced level enjoy. It combines speaking, comprehension, and reasoning. A teacher can choose a controversial, but safe, topic for their class.

Reading Class

ESL teachers assigned to the advanced level can give reading assignments to the students and they can talk about that during the class. For instance, the teacher can take an article from a newspaper or print out an excerpt from the internet and give a copy to the student. The student will be given time to read and understand it before talking about the article/excerpt. Students can also pick out their own articles and provide a copy for the teacher. After reading it, student and teacher discuss the contents of the article. Reading classes include pronunciation, intonation, vocabulary, and reading comprehension. Always ask you student to read the article silently for comprehension and out loud for pronunciation and intonation.

Listening Class

Listening is a crucial part of learning English. When students can't understand what they hear, then their ability to speak in English is also affected. Non-native English speakers will need some time to get used to listening to people talk in English. Once they are familiar with the sound of English words, then their listening comprehension as well as their English speaking skills will improve. For listening classes in the advanced level, a teacher can give the student CNN audio clips, podcasts, and even audio books to study.

The teacher will play the audio file a maximum of two times only and the student can relay whatever he understood from the news clip. In listening classes, the teacher provides the text as well as the audio materials for the student. The teacher will also prepare the listening devices such as speakers, audio player, headphones, etc.

Writing Class

Some students in the advanced level want to learn Business English. For writing classes, you can teach students how to create business letters for every situation. You can teach your student how to write an email, reply to various kinds of letters, file formal written complaints; write a piece for a newspaper column, and many more. You can also teach creative writing to your students.

Whether your student is in the Beginner, Intermediate, or Advanced Level, it can help to ask him on your first meeting what part of English he wants to focus on. Explain that English is a very broad topic and that he should at least have an idea where he should start. Of course, beginner students will need to learn basic vocabulary, simple grammar, reading, speaking, listening, writing, to pronunciation and intonation. But Intermediate and Advanced level students will have an idea about what part of English they need to put more effort into, depending on their plans for the future. Often, this information can become the basis for creating your lesson plans for your students.

Sample Lesson Plan for Advanced Students — Individual Speaking Class

LESSON TITLE:	**HEALTH AND FITNESS**
LESSON OBJECTIVE:	After this class, the student will be able to engage in advanced discussions on health and fitness, as well as contrast ideas using conjunctions.
TARGET AREAS:	Conjunctions
MATERIALS:	Visual Scaffolding: • Photos of sporting activities: *basketball, cycling, football, golf, gymnastics, hockey, rugby, skiing, snowboarding, soccer, swimming, table tennis, tennis, volleyball*

HEALTH AND FITNESS

ACTIVITIES & PROCEDURES:

WARM-UP ACTIVITY:

Show the student photos of various sporting activities and see if they can still remember the vocabulary. Ask the student to describe what is happening in each photo.

basketball	skiing
cycling	snowboarding
football	soccer
golf	swimming
gymnastics	table tennis
hockey	tennis
rugby	volleyball

LESSON PROPER:

PART 1: Speaking Practice

Ask the student the following questions:

1. What are the advantages and disadvantages of doing sports?
2. What do you do to stay healthy?
3. What sports do you like watching? Why?
4. Are there any sports you don't like watching? Why?
5. Do you play any sports? Which ones? How often?
6. Are there any new sports you'd like to learn? Why?
7. Why do you think sports are so popular?
8. Why do you think the top athletes earn so much money? Do you think that's a good thing or a bad thing? Why?

PART 2: Conjunctions

Introduce the following conjunctions:

but	**yet**
however	**nevertheless**
even though	**in spite of**
although	**while**

ASSESSMENT

Ask the student to complete the following sentences using the conjunctions.

1. I don't really like going to the doctor, **but**...
2. Everyone knows it's important to keep fit and stay healthy. **However,** ...
3. **Even though** smoking is very bad for people's health, ...
4. **Although** I try to exercise at least once a week, ...
5. I spend nearly $60 per month on my gym membership, **yet**
6. I've gained nearly 30 pounds in two months. **Nevertheless,** ...
7. **In spite of** the fact that I've been on a diet for three months, ...

8. **While** a hamburger contains more than 300 calories, …

APPLICATION

Ask the student the same questions as in PART 1, but this time encourage them to use a different conjunction in each of their answers.

—End of Lesson—

LESSON TITLE:	VERB + NOUN COLLOCATIONS
LESSON OBJECTIVE:	After this class, students will understand what collocations are and recognize common collocations with *"do"*, *"make"*, *"go"*, and *"give"*.
TARGET AREAS:	Common Collocations
MATERIALS:	• Photos nouns for collocations: *shopping, a dress, dishes, an exercise, a cake, coffee, money, ironing, laundry, a hotel lobby (reservation), a written exercise with a red cross through it (mistake), university lecture, student doing homework*

VERB + NOUN COLLOCATIONS

ACTIVITIES & PROCEDURES:

WARM-UP ACTIVITY:

Show the students the photos and ask them to describe what is going on in each of them. See if they can identify the correct verb and noun to describe the image, e.g. *go shopping, make a reservation.*

LESSON PROPER:

Ask students to place the nouns from each of the photos with its corresponding verb in the table:

MAKE	DO
coffee	
GO	**GIVE**
	a lecture

shopping	a cake	laundry
coffee	homework	a hotel
dishes	money	reservation
an exercise	ironing	a mistake
		a lecture

Explain that words that go together this way are called **collocations,** and they are common in English. See if the students can think of any more examples of collocations.

ASSESSMENT

Complete the following [verb + noun] collocations. Try to make a full sentence of your own.

1. ___ a speech
2. ___ an apology
3. ___ a recommendation
4. ___ a refund
5. ___ an impression on someone
6. ___ the best you can
7. ___ a presentation
8. ___ a break
9. ___ the truth
10. ___ your temper

APPLICATION

Ask the students to write down 10 sentences to describe themselves using some of the collocations from this lesson or any others they can think of. They should then read each of their 10 sentences to the rest of the group.

For example:

- I always try to **do my best.**
- I don't always **tell the truth**.
- I sometimes **lose my temper**.
- I love to **go shopping** with my friends.

—End of Lesson—

Conclusion

A career in ESL teaching can be very rewarding but often many new teachers find it very challenging and at times, frustrating because they begin with unrealistic expectations. Nevertheless, every inexperienced teacher becomes seasoned over time and finds the teaching techniques that they enjoy using. The key is to have patience, determination, and the passion for teaching. It also helps to be equipped with good and effective lesson plans for your classes.

What many teachers don't know is that teaching regular subjects in a regular school is very different to teaching ESL. To teach English to non-native English speakers requires a different type of skill set. Regular schools make use of traditional teaching methods such as lecturing, but these are not effective when it comes to teaching ESL. Teaching ESL makes use of non-conventional, modern methods of teaching to make sure that students learn and understand the English language. But whether you teach in a regular school or in a language school, the common denominator is to always have good lesson plans. Effective lesson plans help to make teaching and learning easier and more organized.

If you would like to start a career in teaching ESL, you won't be disappointed. Most English Academies provide good compensations for their teachers, and once you get the hang of the job, you will see that it can be quite easy and actually enjoyable. This book will help you as you start a career in ESL teaching. With the many useful tips in lesson planning and helpful advice on teaching ESL, you can arrive at your classes prepared and confident and leave knowing that your lesson has been a success.

Made in the USA
Las Vegas, NV
17 May 2022

48922638R10056